Ur
Commune

Beijing

NORTH KOREA

SOUTH
KOREA

JAPAN

Yellow
Sea

Shanghai

MAP OF
CHINA

TAIWAN

Hong Kong

⊓⊓⊓⊓ GREAT WALL

COWBOY
ON THE STEPPES

· S O N G   N A N   Z H A N G ·

Tundra Books

In loving memory of my mother, Zhu Geng Mei

Copyright © 1997 by Song Nan Zhang

Published in Canada by Tundra Books, *McClelland & Stewart Young Readers*, 481 University Avenue, Toronto, Ontario M5G 2E9

Published in the United States by Tundra Books of Northern New York, P.O. Box 1030, Plattsburgh, New York 12901

Library of Congress Catalog Number: 97-60481

Canadian Cataloguing in Publication Data

Zhang, Song Nan, 1942 –
    Cowboy on the steppes

ISBN 0-88776-410-X

1. Herders – Mongolia – Juvenile literature.   2. Mongolia – Social life and customs – Juvenile literature.   3. Mongolia – Description and travel – Juvenile literature.   4. China – History – Cultural Revolution, 1966-1969 – Juvenile literature.   I. Title

DS793.M7Z42 1997   j951.7   C97-930630-2

We acknowledge the support of the Canada Council for the Arts for our publishing program.

Printed and bound in Canada

1 2 3 4 5 6   02 01 00 99 98 97

August 26, 1968

The train let out a long, heart-wrenching bellow. After a series of shudders, the platform of Beijing Central Station started to crawl backward. Thousands of students waved their arms and shouted to their loved ones from the train windows. Choked promises, pleas, words of regret and love – they all became a single, dizzying cry of farewell.

Under the orders of Mao Tse-tung and the Communist Party, we were to embark on a journey into the unknown. I leaned my head against the window, eyes closed, fighting back tears. People around me were not only parting from their families, they were leaving the city they loved, their future, and their dreams.

I called out to no one. The government had forbidden my parents from coming to the station.

August 29, 1968

The train journey north lasted three long days. We finally boarded buses and, when the paved road came to an end, we climbed onto trucks. The bumpy grassland bounced us up and down so hard that even when the trucks stopped moving, our arms and legs continued to shake.

Everything looked so desolate. For hours all we saw was vast sky and endless grassland, and not a trace of a living soul.

Suddenly, a bright horde appeared on the horizon. In an instant, we were surrounded by horsemen dressed in festive colors. As they rode, they waved flags and raised Mao's Red Book high to welcome us. I have never seen such a sight. Our weariness vanished, for they welcomed us like heroes.

Forty of us from Beijing have been assigned to the Ur Commune. None of us can speak a word of Mongolian. We are divided into groups, each with a Mongolian student as translator. The short, skinny, bespectacled fellow assigned to us seems nervous. He told us that his Mongolian name means Revolution.

September 3, 1968

A horse cart left us at the yurt in which we are to live. I could smell the fresh paint of the few pieces of furniture inside. At the entrance stood five shiny, spotless saddles, shoulder-to-shoulder.

There are a few other yurts nearby. A man invited us into one and it's filthy and crowded. The entire interior is black with smoke grease, the result of years of burning cow dung. The only furniture is a chipped cupboard; a scrap of oily carpet lies on the floor. Our host wiped five thick china bowls with a rag. He offered us homemade milk-skin, fried rice and brown sugar. The food was so strange to me that I could barely eat it. Revolution told me later that we had been served holiday food as an honor.

September 7, 1968

For the past few days, we "educated youth" have been cutting hay. I hate it. I want to be a cowboy; to ride horses and round up cattle. I talked with the officials, and I was given permission to move in with Chinba and his wife, Urgan. They are herders and will teach us how to tend cattle.

September 12, 1968

I woke in the night to the sounds of Urgan sobbing and Chinba sighing helplessly beside her in the dim lamplight. I wanted to ask what happened, but I did not know the words.

This afternoon, when we returned from watering the cattle, a long stick with a piece of dark cloth fluttering from it stood in front of the yurt. Revolution told me that Chinba's newborn son had died during the night.

I am overwhelmed. Chinba's only son had died on the very day I moved in, and I had slept on. Revolution explained that doctors and medicines are scarce here. Such deaths are common.

September 15, 1968

Learning to ride was easier than I expected. The hard part was getting a horse. Horses are treasures here. No one was willing to give one up.

   This morning, people were gathered outside our yurt. Gerrss, the head of our work unit, somberly led his favorite horse, a tall gray-maned stallion, through the crowd and handed me the reins. It's so well-trained that it understands his every move. I took Gerrss's hand and promised again and again that I would take care of the animal as if he were my own eyes.

   The Mongolians have so much respect for horse training that they call the animals by the name of the trainer. They've named the stallion Yi Nan's Gray in my honor. I don't know how to thank Gerrss.

September 17, 1968

Nothing is more beautiful than grasslands on a sunny day. The sky is so clear, so close to the earth that I feel I can touch it. And what clouds there are: galloping horses, serene mountains, peaceful rivers . . . At sunset, when the western sky burns, the clouds throw shadows onto the lakes so the earth looks carpeted in gold. The Mongolians know the grasslands so well – the slightest rise and fall, and even the thickness of different grasses – that they can travel even on the darkest night.

   The grasslands can also be cruel. The air was suffocating this morning when I drove the cattle to pasture. Around noon, the sun disappeared. The wind pressed the tall grass into the earth. Pea-sized raindrops turned into walnut-sized hail. Gray reared wildly. I took off the saddle and covered my head with it. Lightning and thunder followed us, almost playfully, wherever we turned. Poor Gray kicked and jumped, dodging the hail. I watched helplessly until the storm finally passed.

September 20, 1968

On the open steppes cattle like to stick together because, alone, they are easy prey for wolves. Today, I drove the cattle to the river. There were other cattle there, and they soon mingled into one big herd. Even for experienced cowboys, separating hundreds of massive creatures from one another is not easy. For me, it is impossible. At the end of the day, when the other cowboys picked out their cattle and rode away, dozens of mine were missing, gone with the other herds. The cowboys just laughed. I need to memorize the faces of my cattle, and soon.

September 26, 1968

Urgan said a wolf had killed a sheep last night. We set off in her oxcart and found the body, much of it eaten, about ten minutes away from the commune. A sheep weighs twice as much as a wolf. I wondered how a wolf could have dragged it so far.

Urgan grinned and told me an old story: "Once upon a time, a curious shepherd named Slern decided he would discover how a wolf could carry off a sheep. One night he hid inside the sheep pen under a sheepskin. Just before dawn, a gray wolf jumped into the pen and caught the sheep by the throat. The wolf used his own tail to sweep the sheep ahead of him." When Urgan realized I believed her, she laughed.

October 11, 1968

Lately, I've been helping Gerrss with his herd, so I left Chinba's yurt and moved in with Gerrss's family. Gerrss always has commune meetings to go to. He also has nine children, a broken oxcart, and a leaking yurt. His wife, Addia, is beautiful and capable. She spent a few years in elementary school, and knows how to read and to deliver calves.

They are kind to me. In return, I help with chores and have started to teach their children how to write in Chinese. When the nine of them line up in front of me, I call them my loyal platoon.

October 14, 1968

A new tent was set up near us today. An old woman moved in. Her heavily-wrinkled face tells the story of a hard life. Everybody calls her Grandma Gammi. Nobody knows her real name. *Gammi* means road in Mongolian. She was found wandering on a road and now the commune takes care of her.

Addia told me that when Gammi was young, she secretly fell in love with the groom of the old Mongolian king. She was to have his child when the Communists reached Mongolia. The king forced the others to flee with him. The groom went to Outer Mongolia with the king, and never returned. Gammi was left behind. The baby died, and Gammi has been alone ever since.

October 23, 1968

I've memorized the faces of the cattle in my herd. Some have bigger horns, some dark rings around their eyes. Each has a different temperment. The other cowboys no longer laugh at me.

A thin layer of snow covers the withered grasslands. It is time for the herds to move to their winter feeding grounds. The winter migration is the longest of all the seasonal moves for the nomadic herders. The yurts have been folded and loaded onto oxcarts for the long journey. Revolution has a herd of sheep, and he left three days ago with them because they move slowly. We started out with the cattle yesterday afternoon. We camped at sunset: the old people, women and children slept on the carts. I slept with the other young men in the snow.

Addia woke me before dawn. The wheels of the carts at the front of the line were already squeaking above the howling wind. The cattle seem to have had enough of the bone-biting cold and follow obediently.

It's just before sunset and we've arrived at the winter camp. A cluster of yurts has been set up, and the crisp air is full of the scent of burning dung and bubbling mutton soup. The smell has grown pleasant to me.

November 14, 1968

Ella, Gerrss's eldest son, and I set out for market in a near-by town as a few shivering rays of morning sun broke through the hazy horizon. We dozed as the ox walked rhythmically up and down the hilly road.

The cart stopped so abruptly that I was nearly tossed off. Just ahead, over the crest, stood a gray wolf with startled eyes. The stand-off between ox and wolf lasted only a few seconds. Then both turned and ran. Only Blacky, Ella's puppy, was undaunted. He charged after the wolf. I jumped off the cart and grabbed him.

November 23, 1968

There are so many people living in Gerrss's place that I crave the quiet of Grandma Gammi's yurt. I often go there to read in peace. I call her Grandma now; the name Gammi brings back bad memories. She lets me sit in the middle of her yurt, a place usually reserved for the head of the household, and serves me her best tea and food. Her two big dogs have accepted me as family. When I am reading, they lie by my sides, heads and paws in my lap.

Maybe because of the long solitude, Grandma talks to everything around her. She tells stories to her dogs, to the cows and sheep, and even to the old wooden cart and the fire on the stove.

November 27, 1968

When I checked my cattle this morning, I found big patches of blood on the ground. Gerrss told me that I must be constantly on guard for wolves now, for as the season changes, the wolves will come in packs.

November 29, 1968

I spend all day in the saddle, circling the herd. Poor Gray has grown thinner. I want to keep him healthy, so this morning I let him loose and tended the herd on foot. Then, as the sun began to slide, I rode around one more time, took off Gray's saddle, loosened his reins and lay down. When I woke, the herd had scattered over the hills. As I was about to remount to collect them, they turned and pounded toward me.

Wolves.

I waved my long stick and charged into the stampeding herd. I counted sixty wolves, navigating their way in and out of the sea of maddened, stomping legs as neatly as seasoned seamen. I shouted and beat at the wolves with all my strength. One by one, I drove them back.

I slid from the horse in exhaustion. The herd stopped the aimless stampede and turned toward me, as if begging me to stand up. They inched closer, bellowing and nodding their heads. I was so moved by their trust that I promised to fight on if the wolves should return.

December 17, 1968

There are few traces of life on the steppes in winter. When I rode up into the hills this morning, I could hear nothing but the tapping of horseshoes on the thin crust of ice. Deep in the valley, an unusually-shaped stone caught my eye. I soon realized it was not a stone – it was a body. Beside it lay a piece of gray brick with strange marks and signs carved into it.

I heard a distant shriek; a sound so piercing, so strange, that it sent shivers through me. I looked around and saw nothing but emptiness. I was about to dismiss the sound as my imagination when another shriek made me kick my horse and race home without looking back.

December 22, 1968

I told Revolution about what I had seen. He said that before the Cultural Revolution, the valley had been a traditional burying ground. Now only a few people keep up the ancient practices. And the shrieks – they were not from ghosts, but from camels. Camels call out to identify themselves to one another. Their high-pitched voices can be heard at great distances.

As for the body, it had been left in the sacred burying ground so that it might go to heaven.

Every three or four days, we exchange our tired horses for fresh ones. Last night I was sent off to fetch rested animals. It took me longer than I expected to harness them. By the time I turned toward home, snow had started to fall from the dark sky.

At first, the flakes were like loosely-falling feathers, soft and gentle, melting on my face. But soon they hardened into stinging arrows. I could barely see the head of my horse. In a matter of minutes, all landmarks had vanished. I rode forever, it seemed, with the other horses tied behind me before I realized I had been circling the same hill. I was lost.

Fear, regret, anger, self-pity, and a dozen other emotions flooded me. Then the emotions faded, replaced by memories. I smelled the earthy scent of the burning dung; I saw Grandma's old oil lamp with its warm flame and I longed for a sip of her steaming milk tea. I thought of my mother and the fairy-tale she had read me long ago in our old house in Beijing, the one about the little girl who froze to death holding on to a burnt-out match.

I pinched myself, shook my head and struggled to keep my eyes open. I knew what it would mean if I fell asleep.

I can't remember how long it was before I saw a flash of light in the distance. As though by instinct, I followed that light. Suddenly a big yurt appeared. The horses jerked to a stop, and I slid to the ground. A man lifted the door flap and looked out. The light I had seen must have come from his yurt.

Late today, when I finally awoke, I was in a stranger's yurt. A woman brewed me a steaming pot of tea. I learned that I was a hundred miles from my own commune.

February 16, 1969

Yesterday I asked Gerrss to look after my herd, and I rode to town to visit my classmates from Beijing. I haven't spoken a full or correct sentence for so long – my Mongolian vocabulary is still so small – that I needed to empty the words stuck in my heart.

My classmates mobbed me, asking about my life as a cowboy. They even prepared a bath for me in a big gasoline barrel. I hadn't bathed since I left them. I was coated in a thick layer of hardened grease and dirt, and I had to use laundry detergent to scrub myself. Later, I joined them by the fire. Life is good!

March 16, 1969

Spring comes first on the wind. The sky is crystal clear again, and skylarks soar free above us. Although there is still a bite in the early morning air, our hearts grow warmer each day.

Every morning there are new calves in the herd. Each new tiny bellow adds to the general happiness. I saw the birth of a calf for the first time. Addia helped the wet calf emerge from the cow. Within minutes, it was trying to stand on its stick legs. The cow couldn't stop licking her baby. When the happy calf found the udders, it drank with such greedy devotion that we all laughed.

Fifty, sixty, seventy; we have been counting new heads. Gerrss can't stop smiling.

March 20, 1969

I finished tending the cattle late tonight. Before I could sit down and have a sip of tea, Grandma yelled at me to come outside. She called me a lazy and callous cowboy. The neighbors glared. At first I did not understand. Grandma insisted that I had let a calf go missing. Addia pulled me away to her yurt and offered me food. I could not swallow it and went straight to sleep.

A few hours later she shook me awake. Outside, I heard the desperate cry of a cow. Addia already had Gray ready. Grandma had been right – one of the calves was missing. The mother was searching for her baby. I could see Grandma already following the cow; her hand-torch flickering ahead of me.

I soon caught up to her. I could hear the cow's bellow clearly. Grandma was gasping for air and could run no further. I had not brought a light but I ran after the sound. Suddenly the cow's cry was echoed by a cry more tender. The mother had found her baby and I had found them both.

What a lucky calf. It is back with its mother – so many people cared about it, worried about it. As for me, I don't even know where my parents are. I don't know when I will ever see them again.

April 5, 1969

The snow and ice are melting. Thousands of clear water lakes have appeared overnight. Flocks of birds pass overhead, searching for dry hay and straw with which to build their nests. I hear an excited skylark open its golden voice to chase away the winter.

I bumped into Chinba early this morning. Urgan is expecting a baby. Chinba was beaming; he hasn't smiled since his son died last year. Hope, like the steppes in spring, is alive again.

April 11, 1969

We are getting ready for the great spring ride. Gerrss has taught me to "hang" Gray – to get him in shape by feeding him less food but giving him plenty of water. He has shown me exercises to turn Gray's winter fat into strong muscle.

April 16, 1969

Just before dawn, all the men and many boys gathered for the ride to drive the wolves back from the herds. For cowboys, the event is more for catching up with old friends than for protecting the herds. Their horses were impeccably groomed, and fitted with gleaming saddles. The elders sat in the center of the throng to draw up the route. Riders proudly patted their animals and made exaggerated claims about how fast and how far their horses can run.

As the sun finally pushed away the mist, the "go" order was given. With the call, it seemed an invisible gate was lifted, and the horses and riders poured onto the plains.

The sounds: whistling, laughter, barking of dogs, and the stomping of hooves pounding so hard that the very earth trembled.

I was caught in the middle of the tide, moving with the shape of the earth. I am no longer afraid. I am a part of this land, this sky, and this people. I am finally a cowboy of the steppes.

EDITOR'S NOTE

In order to quell student unrest in China during the Cultural Revolution, the high school classes of 1966 through 1968 – millions of young people – were forced to leave their homes, their families, and all that was familiar, to work in the countryside. By the end, seventeen million people had been sent to the most remote areas of China to be "reeducated". When Yi Nan was eighteen, he was sent from the bustling, crowded city of Beijing to a place that could not have been more different - the wide, empty expanses of Mongolia. Yi Nan kept detailed diaries during the eight years he lived on the plains, or steppes. His brother, Song Nan Zhang, has added his paintings to describe a year in the life of an unlikely cowboy on the steppes of Inner Mongolia.

Today Yi Nan is the economics editor of the foreign edition of the *People's Daily* in Beijing. He remembers the beautiful landscapes of Mongolia, and the remarkable people who became his friends, with the deepest respect and affection.

RUSSIA

MONGOLIA

INNER
MONGOLIA

INDIA